MAINE

CONTENTS

THE PINE TREE STATE

A Quick Look at
MAINE

State Tree: White Pine

This tough evergreen tree—the source of Maine's Pine Tree State nickname—has been an important part of the state's economy for hundreds of years. The tallest, straightest white pines in the Maine woods were once called "mast pines" because they were perfect for carrying ships' sails. The white pine was made the official state tree in 1945.

State Bird: Chickadee

In 1927, Maine chose the chickadee to be the state bird. This small bird gets its name from its unusual call, which sounds like "chick-a-dee-dee." The black-capped chickadee, about 5 inches (13 centimeters) long, can be seen in wooded areas and backyards of homes throughout the state. The birds do not migrate, so Mainers can hear their cheerful calls all year round.

State Fish: Landlocked Salmon

The landlocked salmon is a freshwater fish that can weigh as much as 35 pounds (16 kilograms). Maine named this salmon its official fish in 1969. It is a natural resident of many of Maine's rivers, streams, and lakes. Maine's oldest recorded landlocked salmon was thirteen years old.

MAINE

WITHDRAWN

Terry Allan Hicks

Amanda Hudson

Cavendish Square

New York

Published in 2014 by Cavendish Square Publishing, LLC
303 Park Avenue South, Suite 1247, New York, NY 10010

Website: cavendishsq.com

This publication represents the opinions and views of the author based on his or her personal experience, knowledge, and research. The information in this book serves as a general guide only. The author and publisher have used their best efforts in preparing this book and disclaim liability rising directly or indirectly from the use and application of this book.

CPSIA Compliance Information: Batch #WS13CSQ

All websites were available and accurate when this book was sent to press.

Library of Congress Cataloging-in-Publication Data
Hicks, Terry Allan.
     Maine / Terry Allan Hicks and Amanda Hudson.—2nd ed.
         p. cm.—(It's my state!)
     Includes bibliographical references and index.
     Summary: "Surveys the history, geography, government, economy, and people of Maine"—Provided by publisher.
     ISBN 978-1-60870-881-9 (hardcover)—ISBN 978-1-62712-094-4 (paperback)—ISBN 978-1-60870-887-1 (ebook)
     1. Maine—Juvenile literature. I. Hudson, Amanda. II. Title.
  F19.3.H53 2013
  974.1—dc23
                                     2012005174

This edition developed for Cavendish Square Publishing by RJF Publishing LLC (www.RJFpublishing.com)
Series Designer, Second Edition: Tammy West/Westgraphix LLC
Editor, Second Edition: Emily Dolbear

Printed in the United States of America

State Cat: Maine Coon Cat

This large cat originated in Maine, probably from different breeds of cat brought over by European settlers. These long-haired cats, larger and heavier than most other pet cats, are perfectly suited to Maine winters. A Maine coon cat also has a bushy tail that it wraps around itself to keep warm, as well as big round paws that serve as snowshoes. Maine coon cats communicate with an unusual trilling sound.

State Animal: Moose

This large brown mammal is the largest member of the deer family in the world. A male moose may be as tall as 6 feet (2 meters) at the shoulders and weigh 1,400 pounds (635 kg). Male moose antlers can spread 5 feet (1.5 m) across. Moose live around Maine's forests and fields and are often seen in backyards. In many parts of the state, "Moose Crossing" signs warn motorists to watch out for them. Maine made the moose its official state animal in 1979.

State Insect: Honeybee

Maine's official state insect is the honeybee. Because the bees pollinate the flowers on plants and trees, the insects are important to orchards, farms, and gardens around the state. Honeybees also make sweet honey used and sold throughout Maine. The honeybee was named the official insect in 1975.

The Pine Tree State

New England is made up of six states in the Northeast: Connecticut, Maine, Massachusetts, New Hampshire, Rhode Island, and Vermont. Maine is the largest of the New England states. Its total land area is 30,843 square miles (79,883 square kilometers)—that is almost as big as all of the other five states put together. This comparatively large state, divided into sixteen counties, is home to a surprisingly small number of people, however. The state population is around 1.3 million, which is smaller than the populations of forty other states. There are large portions of Maine with almost no human residents.

The state's landscape and climate can make it a tough place to live. The coastline is rocky and jagged. The farmland in much of Maine is poor, and the growing season is short. Thick forests cover almost 90 percent of the Pine Tree State—the highest percentage of any state in the nation. The winters are long and bitterly cold. But these harsh conditions have given Maine residents, or Mainers, a reputation for being tough and independent. Many Mainers could not imagine living anywhere else. And many people from outside the state love Maine, too. The Pine Tree State is one of the country's most popular tourist destinations.

Quick Facts

MAINE BORDERS

North	Canada
South	Atlantic Ocean
East	Canada
	Atlantic Ocean
West	New Hampshire
	Canada

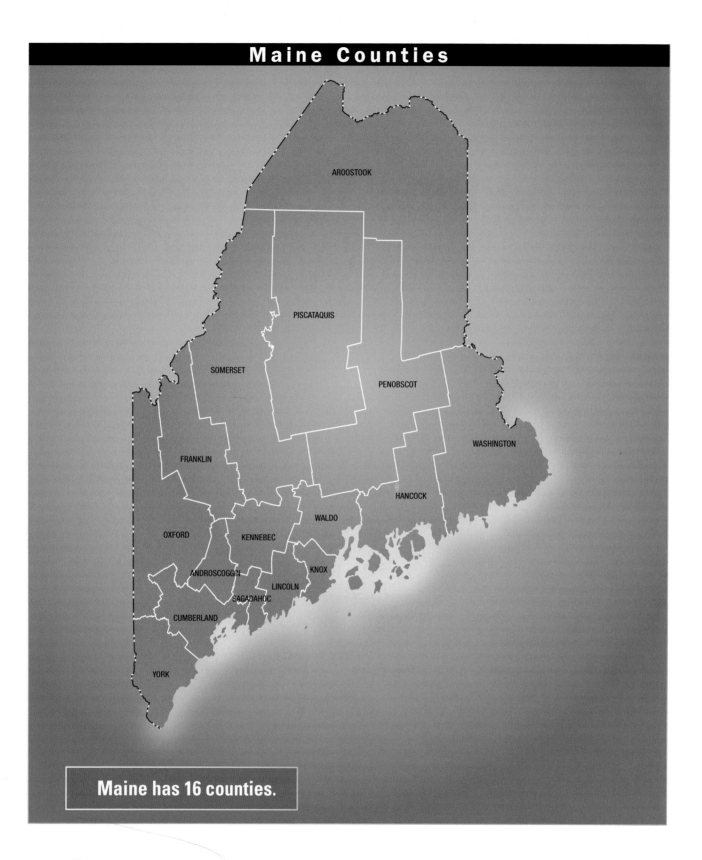

Maine has 16 counties.

The small coastal town of Camden is a popular vacation spot. Its population nearly triples in the summer months.

The Coastal Lowlands

Maine can be divided into three main regions: the Coastal Lowlands, the Eastern New England Uplands, and the Great North Woods. The Coastal Lowlands cover the land that includes Maine's Atlantic coast. If you follow every twist and turn of the Maine coast, it is an amazing 3,478 miles (5,597 km), which is about as long as the California coast. This coastline is Maine's most popular tourist destination. Summer homes line the coast, from the busy sandy beaches in the south to the quieter communities close to the Canadian border. Visitors come here to enjoy the sun and sand at Old Orchard Beach and Ogunquit, eat lobster rolls and fried clams in little seaside restaurants, shop in the outlet stores of Freeport, and photograph fishing villages and lighthouses that are centuries old.

But the Coastal Lowlands are not just a playground. The sleek pleasure boats that glide through the water off the coast pass many working fishing boats. Every day of the year, in good weather and bad, Maine's fishers are hard at work, hauling in lobsters from the offshore waters. "It's year round," said George Johnson, who fished in Maine for more than sixty years. "If you see Maine lobsters for sale in the winter, they're fresh." Maine's fishers also bring in cod and haddock from farther out in the Gulf of Maine.

Acadia National Park covers more than 50 square miles (130 sq km) of Maine's Coastal Lowlands.

When the last Ice Age ended about ten thousand years ago, the retreating glaciers left behind thousands of jagged inlets in the shoreline. The glaciers also created more than two thousand islands, strung out like a jeweled necklace in the waters along the Maine coast. Only a few of these islands—such as North Haven, in Penobscot Bay—are still home to year-round communities.

More than three thousand "summer people" spend part of the year on North Haven. But when the cold weather comes, the island's population drops to about 350. One year-rounder has said, "Island living takes a special kind of person. It's an hour's ride on the ferry just to get to the mainland, so you have to be able to take care of yourself. You also have to know how to get along with people, because this is such a close-knit community. After twelve years here, I really can't imagine a better place to live."

The most famous island in Maine is Mount Desert, home to Acadia National Park, which is the only national park in New England. Mount Desert measures 100 square miles (260 sq km) and is covered with tall peaks, including Cadillac Mountain, which rises up to 1,530 feet (466 m) and is the highest point on the

Atlantic coast of North America. Some people say that if you stand at the top of Cadillac Mountain at daybreak, you will be the first person in the United States to see the sun rise. The town of Bar Harbor is also located on Mount Desert. This town is a popular tourist destination as well as a thriving seashore community.

Almost half of Maine's population lives within about 20 miles (32 km) of the Atlantic Ocean. Portland, the state's largest city with more than 66,000 people, is found on the Atlantic coast, on beautiful, sweeping Casco Bay. Portland has been an important seaport and shipbuilding center for centuries. Today, it also has high-tech industries and an international airport. The greater Portland area, which includes the surrounding towns and cities, has a population of more than 500,000.

Quick Facts

PORTLAND HEAD LIGHT

More than sixty lighthouses are scattered along Maine's coastline. The oldest, Portland Head Light, was first lit in 1791. It still shines brightly today. The lighthouse, along with the museum next to it and nearby Fort Williams Park, are popular with both locals and visitors.

The Eastern New England Uplands

Just a few miles inland from the coast is the beginning of Maine's largest region, the Eastern New England Uplands. Here, the retreating glaciers left behind gently rolling hills, hundreds of rivers and thousands of lakes, and the best farmland in the state.

The Uplands are home to most of Maine's agriculture. The area around Augusta, the state capital, is dotted with apple orchards. In 2010, Maine produced 29 million pounds (13 million kg) of apples. Many dairy farms also dot

Many Maine farms allow customers to pick their own fruit. This farm offers small, flavorful lowbush blueberries.

the Uplands. In the blueberry barrens in the northeastern corner of the state, Mainers harvest bushel after bushel of tiny, delicious wild blueberries.

Maine's most important agricultural area is Aroostook County, which Mainers call the County, along the Canadian border. In this part of the state, many school schedules are arranged around the harvest season. Students are given a "harvest break" in the fall to help with potato farming. The County takes up 6,453 square miles (16,713 sq km), making it Maine's largest county by far. Aroostook County is actually bigger than the states of Connecticut and Rhode Island put together.

The Uplands also have many industrial centers, such as the twin cities of Lewiston and Auburn. These cities face each other from opposite banks of the Androscoggin River. Lewiston is the state's second-largest city. Another important Upland city is Bangor, on the Penobscot River. Bangor is the heart of Maine's all-important lumber industry. For many years, loggers floated fallen trees downriver to Bangor, where they were cut into boards for construction or mashed into pulp for paper.

Tourists come to the Uplands, too, to stay in little cabins, called camps, and fish, hunt, canoe, and hike. Most of Maine's more than two thousand lakes and ponds are found in the Uplands. This includes the biggest of them all, Moosehead Lake. More than three hundred islands can be found on Moosehead Lake, which is 40 miles (64 km) long.

The Great North Woods

To the north and west of the Uplands is the region that shows most clearly why Maine is called the Pine Tree State. This area, the Great North Woods, is mostly untouched by human beings. People have said that, in the North Woods, a tree can grow, live, and die without ever being seen by a human being. The trees grow so thick and close here that, in many places, walking is nearly impossible.

The Longfellow Mountains run down through the heart of this region. These mountains are part of the much-larger Appalachian Range. The highest of the Longfellows is Mount Katahdin. Katahdin is Maine's highest point and rises

Mount Katahdin was named by the Penobscot Indians. *Katahdin* means "the greatest mountain."

Visitors to the Allagash River can camp in designated sites along the waterway. The river is known for its large population of native brook trout.

5,268 feet (1,606 m)—almost 1 mile (1.6 km). Mount Katahdin is surrounded by Baxter State Park, a favorite spot for campers and hikers, and especially for people hiking on the Appalachian Trail. This rugged trail runs for 2,174 miles (3,499 km), down through fourteen states. The trail ends at Springer Mountain in Georgia. An estimated 4 million people hike along different parts of the trail every year.

The Longfellow Mountains are great for winter sports, such as downhill skiing or snowboarding on Sugarloaf Mountain, Maine's second-highest peak. Farther north in the Great North Woods, beyond the mountains, is another of Maine's hidden treasures: the Allagash Wilderness Waterway. The Allagash is a 92-mile (148-km) chain of rivers and lakes that attracts canoeists and white-water kayakers from all over the world. It is also home to Maine's wildest

Quick Facts

THE APPALACHIAN TRAIL

In 1936, a hiker named Myron Avery became the first person to walk the entire length of the Appalachian Trail. He did it in sections over the course of sixteen years. In 2011, a new record was set. Long-distance hiker Jennifer Pharr Davis completed the fastest-ever "thru-hike" of the Appalachian Trail. It took her forty-six days, eleven hours, and twenty minutes.

wildlife. One visitor from Connecticut learned that the hard way, while canoeing on the Allagash with a friend. "We saw a huge rock in the river ahead of us," he remembers. "We were paddling like crazy to keep from hitting it when the 'rock' raised its head, and we realized it was a moose. I don't know who was more surprised—us or him!"

Climate

For six to eight months of the year, Mainers enjoy a pleasant, mild climate. Spring in Maine can be a delight. The summers are usually comfortable, too, with days that are warm but not too hot. Nighttime temperatures can drop suddenly, however, especially along the coast.

Maine residents are accustomed to the state's snowy winters.

Many people believe autumn is the best time to be in Maine. When the temperature begins to fall, the leaves of this heavily wooded state turn to glorious reds, oranges, and yellows. This time of year attracts so-called leaf peepers from all over the world. But a Maine autumn can also have some dangers. Nor'easters are huge, violent storms that blow in from the Atlantic Ocean. These storms sometimes bring hurricane-force winds. When that happens, Mainers know the time has come to tie down their boats, board up the windows of their houses, and wait for the "blow" to end.

There is no doubt about it—you have to be tough to make it through a Maine winter. Maine winters can seem to last forever. In fact, winter weather conditions can last almost six months, from late November to early May. The Maine coast receives about 60 inches (152 cm) of snow during an average winter. Deep in the interior parts of the state, the snowfall is even heavier, at about 100 inches (254 cm).

The winters are cold, too. The average low temperature along the coast in January is 13 degrees Fahrenheit (–11 degrees Celsius). Inland, especially in the northern parts of the state, it is even colder. The average January low for Caribou, near the Canadian border, is 1 °F (–17 °C). Maine's rivers and lakes ice over, and it sometimes seems as if the state comes to a standstill, just waiting for spring.

Wildlife

About half of Maine is completely uninhabited, which helps make the state ideal for wildlife. The skies above the coast are filled with hundreds of different species (types) of birds, from bald eagles and ospreys to cormorants and puffins. The waters along the coast and around the offshore islands are home to several different kinds of seals. And below the surface of the water are lobsters, crabs, clams, mussels, scallops, shrimps, and sea urchins. The many species of fish include cod, flounder, and mackerel. A little farther out in the ocean, it is not unusual to see porpoises and whales breaking the surface.

The mainland is home to a wonderful variety of wildlife—especially in the North Woods, far from civilization. Here, in the thick evergreen forests, black bears search for mountain cranberries, while moose nibble on water plants, and white-tailed deer shelter their young. The few people who travel through the woods may also see beavers, porcupines, snowshoe hares, and bobcats.

Whale-watching cruises are a popular attraction along the Maine coast.

The golden eagle is one of Maine's rarest birds. The wingspan of this bird can reach 6 feet (2 m).

This heavily forested state is covered with balsam, beech, birch, maple, oak, and of course, pine trees. In the spring and summer, many parts of Maine are carpeted with wildflowers, including the black-eyed Susan, the lady's slipper, and a favorite of Mainers, the tall, colorful lupine. For those who know how to properly identify edible wild plants, some of Maine's plant life, including blueberries, cranberries, and fiddlehead ferns, can be very tasty.

The people of Maine live very close to nature, so they care deeply about preserving their natural environment. Mainers have created many laws and regulations to protect the land and wildlife of their state. However, many of Maine's species—from the golden eagle to the box turtle—are endangered (in danger of becoming extinct or completely dying out). Continuing efforts to protect the environment and Maine wildlife will help save the state's endangered species.

Plants & Animals

Atlantic Puffin

These unusual-looking seabirds, with their big blue, red, and yellow beaks, almost disappeared from Maine in the 1800s. People hunted Atlantic puffins for their feathers, which were used in women's hats, and the puffins' food sources, which include herring and shellfish, became scarce from overfishing. But beginning in 1973, a plan called Project Puffin brought baby puffins to live on some of Maine's offshore islands. Today, puffin-watching cruises are a popular way to view these now-plentiful birds.

Black Bear

Black bears may reach 600 pounds (270 kg) and measure 6 feet (2 m) in length. But they can run surprisingly fast—up to 25 miles (40 km) per hour. Black bears are very good tree-climbers. They feed on fish, nesting birds, blueberries, and wild honey in the Maine woods. They have also been known to help themselves from residential bird feeders and garbage cans.

Lupine

One of Maine's best-known symbols, these tall wildflowers can be found throughout the state's forests and fields. Lupines are commonly deep purple, lavender, pink, or white. Deer Isle holds a lupine festival every June, when the flowers are at their peak.

Harbor Seal

Harbor seals were once threatened (at risk of becoming endangered) in Maine. The large mammals competed with fishers for valuable fish such as herring and scallops, and they were believed to eat bait from lobster traps. From 1905 until 1962, hunters were awarded one dollar for every seal they killed. But environmental laws now help protect these migratory mammals, and today harbor seals live in almost every harbor along Maine's coast.

Canada Lynx

This shy predator, known for black tufts of fur on its ears, is one of the rarest sights in the Maine woods. Although the Canada lynx is considered a threatened species, some experts think its population may be as large as 1,200 when there are larger numbers of snowshoe hares to feed on. The Canada lynx looks similar to a bobcat, with longer legs.

Lichen

Lichens are plantlike organisms made up of fungi, algae, and bacteria. They grow on trees, rocks, and fence posts throughout the Maine woods. Lichens need only light, air, and moisture to survive, so they can often live where almost no other life forms could. Many of Maine's wild animals, such as moose, birds, and deer, feed on lichen.

Celebrating Maine's
Native American Heritage

ABBE
MUSEUM

ABBE MUSEUM

CELEBRATING MAINE'S NATIVE AMERICAN HERITAGE

From the Beginning

People have lived in the land we now know as Maine for thousands of years. Very little is known about the first of these early American Indians, who are called Paleo-Indians. But they probably hunted caribou and other large animals by using stone weapons. Archaeologists have found stone tools dating back to around this time.

A new group of American Indians appeared around 2500 BCE. They are known as the Red Paint People because they buried their dead in elaborate graves colored with red pigment. They seem to have disappeared by about 1800 BCE. Centuries later, probably around 700 CE, another group of American Indians lived along the coast. These people were probably fishers. They are known as "ceramic people" because of the clay vessels they left behind.

The People of the Dawn

By the fourteenth century—and perhaps much earlier—present-day Maine was home to a new group of American Indians, the Abenaki. The name *Abenaki* means "people of the dawn." The Abenaki are part of the much larger Algonquian group, which includes tribes that traditionally lived throughout New England and other areas of northern North America.

Many different Abenaki groups lived in what is now Maine, including the Penobscot, the Passamaquoddy, the Maliseet, and the Micmac. There were many

The Abbe Museum in Bar Harbor has collections that represent ten thousand years of American Indian culture and history in Maine.

The Abenaki lived in small homes made of birch bark called wigwams.

differences among these groups. The Passamaquoddy, who lived in northeastern Maine, were mostly hunters. The Penobscot were farmers, growing corn and beans on the fertile farmland of the central coast.

For centuries, the Abenaki fought their traditional enemies, the Iroquois, who lived to the north and the west of them. By the 1600s, war had weakened the Abenaki, making it difficult for them to face a new threat—the arrival of the Europeans.

Explorers and Settlers

Historians debate which Europeans were the first to visit Maine. Some believe it was the Vikings, who were warriors originally from Norway and Denmark. After reaching Greenland, they sailed their longships down the east coast of North America, perhaps as early as 1000 CE.

Beginning in the 1500s or shortly before, other European explorers began visiting what is now Maine. Giovanni Caboto (also known as John Cabot), an Italian sea captain who sailed for England, may have traveled along the coast in 1497. Historians have never been able to agree on his landing site. In 1524, another Italian explorer, Giovanni da Verrazzano, landed at Casco Bay, near present-day Portland. Because his ship was owned by France, he claimed the land for the French. Early European visitors described Maine as beautiful but dangerous. Tension between Verrazzano and the Abenaki led to his calling the region "the Land of Bad People."

The first European attempt to settle in present-day Maine ended in disaster. In 1604, Pierre du Guast—part of a French expedition led by the explorer Samuel de Champlain—built a small outpost on an island at the mouth of the Saint Croix River. The French called the island Île des Monts Déserts. Today, it is known as Mount Desert Island. Champlain went up the Penobscot River, as far as where Bangor is today. When he returned the following spring, he found more than half of Guast's crew dead or dying, most from a disease called scurvy, which is caused by a diet lacking in vitamin C. The outpost was abandoned.

The French never again tried to settle in Maine, but they did not really leave, either. They traded extensively with the Abenaki for animal furs, which were very popular in Europe. The French became the Abenaki's most important trading partners and closest allies. This would later cause great problems with the next group to settle in Maine—the English.

The scenic Popham Beach State Park is located in Phippsburg. The site is named in honor of George Popham, cofounder of Maine's first English settlement.

A Century of War

The English were living in what is now Maine as early as 1607, when Captains Raleigh Gilbert and George Popham established a colony near the mouth of the Kennebec River. The Popham Colony, as it is now known, was established in August and hit hard by its first brutal winter. Many of the colonists died, including Popham. In 1608, Gilbert and the remaining colonists sailed back to England.

In 1622, the English king, James I, granted a large piece of land in New England to two English nobles, Sir Ferdinando Gorges and John Mason. Seven years later, the two men split up the land, with Gorges taking the northern section, which was the part that became Maine. Mason's share is now the state

NAME OF MAINE

Some people think early explorers named the Pine Tree State after the former French province of Maine. Others think it came from Sir Ferdinando Gorges, who lived near the English village of Broadmayne. Or it may have gotten its name because it is "the mainland," not the coastal islands.

of New Hampshire. In 1652, the small, scattered English settlements of Maine came under the control of the older, more established Massachusetts Bay Colony.

The English soon came into conflict with the French, who also wanted to control Maine and its rich resources. In 1689, the English began fighting the first of a long series of wars against the French and their Abenaki allies. These conflicts, sometimes known as the Colonial Wars, lasted almost a century.

Life was hard for the early European settlers of Maine, but it was far harder for the American Indians. Europeans brought diseases to which Indians had no resistance. From 1616 to 1619, disease wiped out a large portion of their population. This time period is now known as the "Great Dying." Later, many Abenaki fled the French-English fighting to live in French-controlled areas in Canada.

The last of the Colonial Wars was the French and Indian War (1754–1763), between France and its Indian allies, including the Abenaki, and Great Britain and its Indian allies. Many Abenaki were killed in this conflict, which was won by the British. As a result, the French signed an agreement that gave Britain control of virtually all the land France had claimed in eastern North America.

TALL TREES FOR THE BRITISH

Great Britain ruled its American colonies with many laws. One British law that Mainers hated was the mast preservation law. According to this law, the area's largest white pines belonged to the king—to be used as masts for British navy ships. Government-appointed "mast agents" marked the trees that the colonists were not permitted to cut down.

By the time the French and Indian War came to an end, thousands of British colonists were living in Maine. Settlers were moving farther inland, clearing the forests to create farmland. There was a period of peace in Maine, but it did not last long.

More Wars

By the 1770s, many people in Britain's American colonies were ready to be free of British rule. The colonists had to pay taxes on many items, including tea, but they felt they had no voice in their government. Opposition to British rule led to the American Revolution (1775–1783).

Mainers played an important role before and during the war. They burned British tea shipments in York in 1774, in an incident known as the York Tea Party. When the American Revolution started in 1775, the people of Maine fought hard on the side of independence. The first naval battle of the war was in June 1775, around the port of Machias, when Mainers seized a British ship called the *Margaretta*. The Mainers used their knowledge of the land to their advantage. They sometimes extinguished the signals in the lighthouses along the coast, which caused British ships to run onto the rocks.

Maine paid a high price for its actions against the British. In October 1775, the British attacked the city of Falmouth, now Portland, to punish the colonists for their acts of rebellion. In what is now called the Burning of Falmouth, hundreds of buildings were burned to the ground, and most of the ships in the harbor were sunk. When the war ended in 1783—with an American victory and independence—Maine worked hard to recover. Falmouth was rebuilt. Maine's shipyards hummed with activity, as timber from the state's pine forests was used to make wooden sailing ships.

Many new settlers arrived in Maine. Huge pieces of land—totaling about 12.5 million acres (5 million hectares)—were taken from the Passamaquoddy and Penobscot Indians and given to soldiers who had fought in the American Revolution. For a time, the region was prosperous and peaceful. But once again, Maine's good times were shattered by war. Mainers were almost as unhappy

The Burning of Falmouth in 1775, during the American Revolution, resulted in the destruction of more than four hundred buildings.

with the state government in Massachusetts as they had been with their British rulers. This turned into great bitterness during a conflict between Britain and the new United States called the War of 1812.

The British took control of a long stretch of the northern Maine coast, from Belfast to Eastport, close to the Canadian border. They cut off all contact with the outside world, and the Maine economy suffered terribly. Maine asked Massachusetts for help—but no help came. The War of 1812 officially ended in 1814.

Statehood

After the War of 1812, the people of Maine demanded statehood. They got their wish on March 15, 1820. Maine became the twenty-third state in the

Logging has been an important part of Maine's history. Mainers have used lumber for shipbuilding, construction, pulp, and paper.

A COMPROMISE

Maine's statehood in 1820 came as part of an agreement in the U.S. Congress that became known as the Missouri Compromise. At the time, there were eleven free states (states that did not allow slavery) and eleven slave states in the young country. The Missouri Compromise called for Maine to enter the Union (another name commonly used for the United States at the time) as a free state and Missouri as a slave state. With this compromise, the numbers of free and slave states remained equal and helped balance power between the North and the South.

United States. Portland was named its capital. In 1832, the capital was moved to Augusta, which is closer to the center of the state and remains the capital today.

The new state was bustling with life. Ships from all over the world filled Maine's harbors, their cargo holds waiting to carry away the state's products: fish, timber, and stone. They even carried blocks of ice—cut from frozen rivers and packed in sawdust to keep from melting—to keep food cold in the days before refrigerators.

By the mid–1800s, mill towns were springing up all over the Maine Uplands. The rushing waters of the Androscoggin and other rivers powered sawmills, textile mills, and shoe factories. The mills employed immigrants, who were beginning to arrive in Maine in large numbers for the first time. Many of these immigrants came from Canada. Life was good for many Americans until the Civil War (1861–1865) began.

AROOSTOOK WAR

In 1839, the United States and Britain almost went to war yet again. This time, it was over the boundary between northern Maine and British-owned Canada. The Treaty of Paris, the peace agreement that ended the American Revolution in 1783, had not clearly defined the boundary of this timber-rich region. A treaty ended the so-called Aroostook War, which never actually escalated into a military conflict, in 1842.

MAKING PUNCHED-TIN ART

Many New England settlers decorated their homes with objects made out of punched tin, such as lanterns or candleholders. They also hung punched-tin pictures on their walls. Following these simple instructions, you can make your own punched-tin art.

WHAT YOU NEED

Piece of plain paper

Pen

Aluminum pie plate

Cellophane or masking tape

Hammer

Nail

You will need an adult to help you use the hammer and nail for this project.

Use a pen to draw a simple design or picture on the piece of paper. Make sure your design will fit within the outside edge of the bottom of the pie plate.

Tape the paper to the pie plate, making sure your design is centered.

Put the pie plate on a work surface, such as a large scrap of wood or very thick cardboard. Ask an adult for help finding a place to put the pie plate so you do not damage the floor, a table, or a countertop.

With an adult's help, punch holes into the pie plate with the hammer and nail. You should follow the lines of your design. The holes should be spaced about ½ inch (1 cm) apart. Work carefully with the hammer and nail.

Remove the paper and display your artwork. You might want to hang it against a window, where light will shine through your design. Everyone will admire your creative piece of punched-tin art.

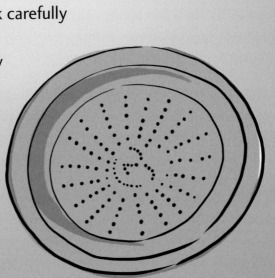

The Civil War

In the 1850s, Americans remained divided over the issue of slavery. Many states, especially in the South, allowed whites to own African Americans as slaves. But most New Englanders did not agree with this practice. The fight against slavery became an important cause for millions of Americans.

Some people believe one of the turning points in the debate over slavery came when a woman in Brunswick, Maine, sat down to write a book. Her name was Harriet Beecher Stowe, and the book, published in 1852, was *Uncle Tom's Cabin*. This novel described the mistreatment of southern plantation slaves and their attempts to escape to the free states in the North. Many publishers were reluctant to publish such a controversial tale. Only 5,000 copies of the first edition were printed. The books sold out in two days. By the end of the year, *Uncle Tom's Cabin* had sold more than 300,000 copies. The novel helped open many people's eyes to the evils of slavery.

In 1861, when the North and South could not resolve their differences, they finally went to war. The Civil War lasted four long years and cost nearly 400,000 Americans their lives.

An estimated 70,000 Mainers fought on the Northern, or Union, side. At the Battle of Gettysburg in 1863, the Twentieth Maine Regiment, outnumbered two to one by the Southern forces, fought until they ran out of ammunition. Then, they charged with bayonets, forcing the Southerners to retreat. This turned the

The Twentieth Maine Regiment defended the hill known as Little Round Top at the Battle of Gettysburg in 1863. A monument to those soldiers is featured at the Gettysburg National Military Park in Pennsylvania.

tide in one of the largest and most important battles of the Civil War. Though none of its battles were fought in Maine, the Civil War took a terrible toll on the state. More than 7,000 of Maine's young men died serving their country.

Time of Growth

The years after the war brought great changes to Maine. The age of the wooden sailing ship was coming to an end, as these vessels were replaced by metal ships powered by steam. The demand for Maine timber decreased. But Mainers adapted. The state's shipyards, especially in Bath, near the mouth of the Kennebec River, began building metal ships, and they still do today.

Maine found new uses for its trees, too. Books and newspapers were becoming more common—because more people knew how to read—and their publishers needed a steady supply of paper. Pulp and paper mills were built all

BATH IRON WORKS
The Bath Iron Works shipyard launched its first ship in 1890. Since then, more than 425 new vessels have been built at the shipyard, including 245 U.S. Navy ships.

across northern Maine, to crush wood into pulp and then turn it into paper. Many of these mills are still in operation.

These growing industries needed more and more workers, and most of them came from other countries. Many of these immigrants came from Ireland, and they gave many places in Maine Irish names, such as Belfast. Others came from Sweden to clear farmland in Aroostook County, and from Finland to work in the stone quarries along the coast. In 1870, fifty-one Swedish immigrants built a town in Aroostook County. The colony of New Sweden expanded to create the neighboring towns of Westmanland, Stockholm, and others.

The largest group of new arrivals came from land much closer to Maine—the nearby Canadian provinces of New Brunswick and Quebec. These French-speaking immigrants mostly came to work in mills and factories. For many years, the French Canadians of Maine kept themselves somewhat separate from other Mainers, living and working in *petits Canadas*, or "little Canadas," with their own schools, churches, and businesses.

During this time, Maine's tourist industry was beginning to grow. The town of Bar Harbor, on Mount Desert Island, was a popular destination for writers and artists. By 1870, Bar Harbor had sixteen hotels. Some had two-year waiting lists for reservations. In the 1880s, the area became a fashionable summer resort, with huge seaside mansions. Summer residents of these Bar Harbor "cottages" included members of the famous Rockefeller and Vanderbilt families.

Soon, steamships and railways began to bring in less wealthy visitors. They first came to spend summers on the coast, in places such as Kennebunk and Camden. Then, resorts began to open on Moosehead and other lakes in the interior. Maine's resorts began to be an important source of jobs for Mainers.

Modern Maine

By the beginning of the twentieth century, Maine's population had grown to about 700,000. As newcomers to the state, both immigrants and "summer people," became more common, Mainers worried about how to preserve the things that made their state special. This has been one of Maine's greatest concerns ever since.

The new century was not always easy for Maine. In 1917, when the United States entered World War I (1914–1918), Maine sent about 35,000 soldiers to fight on the battlefields of Europe. During the war, the state worked to supply the war effort. But after the war, the supplies were no longer needed, causing economic hardship in the state.

In the 1880s, Bar Harbor, shown here in an 1895 illustration, became a fashionable resort town, marking the beginning of Maine's tourist industry.

In Their Own Words

Monuments decay, buildings crumble and wealth vanishes, but Katahdin in its massive grandeur will forever remain the mountain of the people of Maine. Throughout the ages it will stand as an inspiration to the men and women of the state.

—Percival P. Baxter,
fifty-third governor of Maine

It was during this period that the people of Maine first began taking steps to protect their natural environment. In 1919, the U.S. Congress created Lafayette National Park, which was later renamed Acadia National Park. It was the first national park east of the Mississippi River. Beginning in 1931, Percival P. Baxter, a former governor, began donating thousands of acres of land around Mount Katahdin. This wilderness area became Baxter State Park.

But in the 1920s and 1930s, Mainers were mostly concerned with economic survival. Times were hard, and they worsened during the Great Depression. This period of economic hardship, beginning with a stock market crash in 1929, created poverty and unemployment all over the country.

During the Depression, the federal government created a program called the Civilian Conservation Corps (CCC). The CCC was designed to provide jobs for young men during this time of unemployment and poverty. In Maine, the CCC employed about 20,000 people building public works projects, such as hiking trails through the North Woods. CCC workers completed the Appalachian Trail in 1937. In 1999, Maine's legislature established a memorial to the people who served in the CCC.

In the early 1940s, Maine's economy began to improve. In 1941, the United States had entered World War II (1939–1945), which increased demand for the state's natural resources and manufactured goods. The shipyards of the coast were working day and night, as welders and mechanics built destroyers at the Bath Iron Works and submarines at the Portsmouth Naval Shipyard, which was considered part of New Hampshire at the time.

Many of Maine's businesses were forced to close during the Great Depression, which began in 1929.

For several decades after World War II ended, Maine's economy was strong, and the state's workers had little trouble finding jobs. But then, in the late 1970s, that began to change. The traditional Maine industries faced growing competition from other parts of the country, and other parts of the world. Many of the state's factories were moved to places where costs for materials and labor were lower. Two important concerns of Mainers—making a living and protecting the environment—began to come into conflict.

Environmentalists had been pushing for laws to protect Maine's land and wildlife for a long time. But many Mainers worried that these laws would cost jobs. In the 1970s, for example, the state banned clear-cutting, a logging method that cuts down all the trees in an area, along Maine's rivers. It was thought to be harmful to the fish, especially the landlocked salmon. But when environmentalists tried to stop clear-cutting everywhere in the state in 1996, the proposal was defeated. Many people were afraid it would hurt the lumber industry—and put more Mainers out of work.

Quick Facts

BORDER DISPUTE

Strange as it may sound, modern Maine had a border dispute with its only New England neighbor. For more than two centuries, New Hampshire claimed the Portsmouth Naval Shipyard, at the mouth of the Piscataqua River, as part of its land. In 2001, the U.S. Supreme Court ended the controversy by ruling that it belonged to Maine. Today, the shipyard's location is listed as Kittery, Maine.

The Maine economy continues to face some tough times today. More jobs were lost in the state during the nationwide recession that began in late 2007. By 2012, Maine's unemployment rate had recovered to around 7 percent— slightly lower than the average for the rest of the country. The town of East Millinocket, hit especially hard by the recession, breathed a sigh of relief when one of its paper mills was reopened earlier in the year. But various industries, from agriculture to manufacturing, are struggling. Many Mainers are still worried about their jobs. Many are also worried about preserving the natural environment and the traditional Maine way of life. But with time and effort, Mainers will find a way to endure and progress as they have for centuries.

Important Dates

★ **2500** BCE Early American Indians called the Red Paint People appear in the Maine area.

★ **700** CE American Indians known as "ceramic people" begin to live in Maine, along the coast, followed by the Abenaki.

★ **1000–1524** European navigators, including Vikings and the Italians Giovanni Caboto and Giovanni da Verrazzano, sail along the Maine coast.

★ **1607** The Popham Colony is established near the mouth of the Kennebec River.

★ **1622** King James I of England grants "the province of Maine" to Sir Ferdinando Gorges and John Mason, who divide it into Maine and New Hampshire in 1629.

★ **1689–1763** The English fight the French and their American Indian allies in a series of wars.

★ **1774** In York, Mainers burn tea shipped from Britain to protest British taxes on the colonies.

★ **1775** The American Revolution comes to Maine, with a naval engagement in Machias.

★ **1820** Maine becomes the twenty-third state, with Portland as its capital.

★ **1832** Maine establishes Augusta as its capital city.

★ **1861–1865** Maine fights on the Union side in the Civil War.

★ **1929** Lafayette National Park on Mount Desert Island is enlarged and renamed Acadia National Park.

★ **1937** Federal government crews complete the Appalachian Trail.

★ **1948** Margaret Chase Smith of Maine is elected to the U.S. Senate.

★ **1980** The federal courts award the Penobscot and Passamaquoddy tribes $81.5 million for the land taken from them after the American Revolution.

★ **2001** A U.S. Supreme Court ruling returns the Portsmouth Naval Shipyards to Maine, ending a long dispute with New Hampshire.

★ **2009** A record low temperature for Maine, –50 °F (–46 °C), is set at Big Black River.

The People

Maine's long history has given it strong traditions and customs. Mainers are very proud of the Pine Tree State. The hardships of life in Maine have made many of the state's communities very close-knit. People in Maine tell stories of residents plowing their neighbors' driveways during heavy snowfalls, or bringing food to the elderly during power outages. The state's harsh winters mean that neighbors—perhaps more so than in other parts of the country—come to rely on each other.

In some ways, Maine is less diverse than many other states. About 95 percent of Mainers are white. The largest single ethnic group in the state is people of British ancestry, just as it has been since the eighteenth century.

But this does not mean that everybody in the Pine Tree State is the same. One of the largest ethnic groups in the state is people of French-Canadian ancestry.

Quick Facts

ACADIAN EXPULSION

In 1755, French Canadians began settling in Maine's St. John Valley. The British had forced them to leave their homes in New Brunswick and Nova Scotia, which they called Acadia. Many other Acadians went to Louisiana, where they became known as Cajuns. Now known as the Acadian Expulsion, these events inspired Maine poet Henry Wadsworth Longfellow to write "Evangeline, A Tale of Acadie," published in 1847.

Visitors and local residents enjoy summer festivals of all kinds throughout Maine.

Many of Maine's residents are of French-Canadian descent.

To this day, you will hear French spoken, with a Canadian accent, on the streets of Lewiston and Biddeford. Maine's French Canadians have worked hard to preserve their traditional language and culture, and their historical ties with Canada. Some of the highlights of a summer visit to Maine are festivals that celebrate the vibrant French-Canadian culture, with fiddle music, folk dancing, and food.

American Indians

One ethnic group that has had a very difficult time in Maine is the American Indians. Before Europeans

Penobscot and Passamaquoddy leaders visit the Maine legislature in Augusta to represent their tribes in 2002.

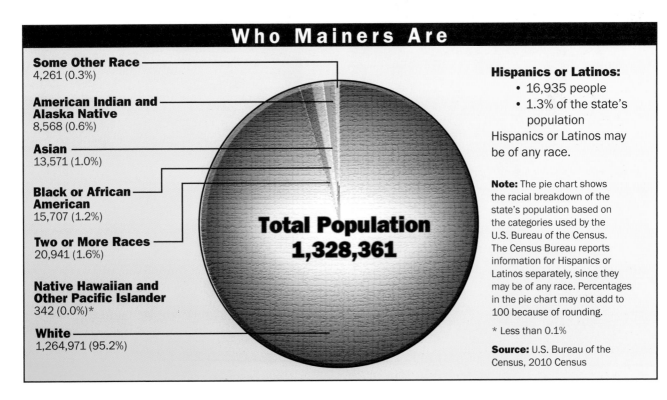

Who Mainers Are

Some Other Race
4,261 (0.3%)

American Indian and Alaska Native
8,568 (0.6%)

Asian
13,571 (1.0%)

Black or African American
15,707 (1.2%)

Two or More Races
20,941 (1.6%)

Native Hawaiian and Other Pacific Islander
342 (0.0%)*

White
1,264,971 (95.2%)

**Total Population
1,328,361**

Hispanics or Latinos:
- 16,935 people
- 1.3% of the state's population

Hispanics or Latinos may be of any race.

Note: The pie chart shows the racial breakdown of the state's population based on the categories used by the U.S. Bureau of the Census. The Census Bureau reports information for Hispanics or Latinos separately, since they may be of any race. Percentages in the pie chart may not add to 100 because of rounding.

* Less than 0.1%

Source: U.S. Bureau of the Census, 2010 Census

The residents of Maine's largest city, Portland, come from all over the world, making it an increasingly diverse place to live.

came to the region, the entire population was American Indian. Now, American Indians make up less than one percent of Maine's population. Many of the Abenaki of Maine live on reservations with high unemployment and poor living conditions. But in recent years, they have worked hard to improve the standard of living on their reservations, as well as to revive their language and their traditional crafts.

Not all of Maine's American Indians live on reservations, of course. Many live in cities and towns all over the state. Wherever they live, these populations continue to honor their heritage through traditional celebrations and festivals held throughout Maine.

New Arrivals

Despite the arrival of French Canadians and others, Maine still has fewer immigrants than most states. But that, like many things about Maine, is changing. In Portland, especially, new arrivals from other countries are beginning to transform the city's downtown area. People from countries as far away as Yemen, Iran, Somalia, and Vietnam are bringing their own cultures and traditions to the state. They open shops, restaurants, and other businesses. A city that once consisted almost entirely of people of European ancestry is now home to people from around the world. Changes are not happening just on the seacoast. Cities and towns inland also have newcomers from other countries. Many people from other states have made Maine their home, too.

Changing Times

People sometimes say there are really two Maines. What they mean is that the seacoast is, in some ways, very different from the interior. The most important difference is in economic opportunity, with more jobs available along the coast.

The seacoast has always been more prosperous than the inland areas of the state, partially because it has more contact with the outside world. In recent years, the division between these two Maines has become even greater than in the past. Many wealthy people have moved to the seacoast, bringing more money to the region, while the resource-based industries of the interior have declined. The result is that the people who live on the seacoast have more job opportunities, and the jobs tend to pay better.

This has caused a significant change in the state's population levels. Maine's overall population has increased steadily for hundreds of years. But in some parts of northern Maine, such as Aroostook and Androscoggin counties, the population is now declining. Young people from these areas often have to move elsewhere to find good jobs.

Even on the seacoast, the arrival of more people, and the money they bring with them, is forcing Mainers to make difficult choices. A landowner may be tempted to sell property that has belonged to his or her family for generations, because the demand for land in some regions is so great. The pressure is especially strong along the waterfront. A small home on waterfront property may sell for millions of dollars. When these houses are sold, they are often torn down to make way for larger, more valuable summer homes.

Educational Opportunities

Some Mainers worry about educational inequality in the state. Schools in wealthier cities and towns along the seacoast can afford more things, such as up-to-date computers, than schools in poorer areas of the state. One program has attempted to bring the "two Maines" together by promoting technology.

In 2002, then-governor of Maine Angus King began an ambitious project to help bridge this "digital divide." The project, the Maine Learning Technology Initiative, is a partnership with Apple Inc. that gives every middle school student his or her own personal laptop computer. At the time it was initiated, the $37.2 million contract was believed to be the largest educational technology purchase by any state. In addition to the computers, the contract included the installation of wireless Internet access in 241 middle schools, as well as technical support.

"Maine's academic standards have done a better job of integrating technology than almost every other state," said Ed Coughlin, a consultant who helped write

Tenth graders in Guilford use laptop computers supplied by the school as part of Maine's initiative to reduce educational inequalities.

Apple's contract proposal. "They have a level of thoughtfulness not common in most state departments of education." In 2009, this successful program was expanded to include high schools. The project shows the state's commitment to providing equal opportunities for all students.

Famous Mainers

Henry Wadsworth Longfellow: Poet

Henry Wadsworth Longfellow is one of the best-known American poets. Longfellow, born in Portland in 1807, grew up in Maine. He also attended Bowdoin College in Brunswick. His first published poem, "The Battle of Lovell's Pond," was printed in the *Portland Gazette* in 1820. Many of Longfellow's works, such as "The Song of Hiawatha" and "The Courtship of Miles Standish," are considered American masterpieces. Longfellow died in 1882.

Hannibal Hamlin: Politician

Hannibal Hamlin was born in 1809 in Paris, Maine. Hamlin was the first Mainer to become vice president of the United States. In the 1840s, he served in the U.S. House of Representatives and the Senate. Hamlin was opposed to slavery and was chosen to run as Abraham Lincoln's vice presidential candidate in the 1860 presidential election. Lincoln was elected, and Hamlin served as his vice president until March 1865. He died in 1891.

Margaret Chase Smith: Politician

Margaret Chase Smith was born in Skowhegan in 1897. Her husband, Clyde Smith, was a politician and she worked as his administrative assistant. After her husband's death in 1940, Smith won her own seat in the U.S. House of Representatives. In 1948, after four terms in the House, she was elected to the U.S. Senate. This made her the first woman elected to both houses of the U.S. Congress. Smith, awarded the Presidential Medal of Freedom in 1989, died in 1995.

Stephen King: Writer

Best-selling author Stephen King was born in Portland in 1947 and has lived almost his entire life in Maine. He has published more than fifty books, which have sold approximately 350 million copies. Many of his novels and short stories have been made into popular movies, such as *The Shawshank Redemption* and *Stand by Me*. Most of his best-known books—including *Carrie*, *Cujo*, and *Under the Dome*—are set in Maine. In 2003, King was honored with the National Book Foundation Medal for Distinguished Contribution to American Letters.

Joan Benoit Samuelson: Athlete

One of Maine's most famous athletes, Joan Benoit Samuelson, was born in 1957 in Cape Elizabeth and attended Bowdoin College. She won the Boston Marathon twice as well as a gold medal at the 1984 Olympic Games in the first women's marathon. One year later, she won the Chicago Marathon. Today, she works for many charitable causes and coaches runners of all ages. Samuelson has also established a world-class road race in her home state, which benefits many of Maine's children's charities.

Patrick Dempsey: Actor

Born in Lewiston in 1966, Patrick Dempsey was a well-known local athlete. He won the Maine State Slalom Championship when he was in high school. His main passion was acting, however. In the 1980s, he earned parts in such movies as *Can't Buy Me Love* and *Happy Together*. In all, Dempsey has acted in more than forty films, but he is perhaps best-known for his television role as Dr. Derek Shepherd on *Grey's Anatomy*.

Three Boys in a Dory, painted by Winslow Homer in 1873, is one of the Maine artist's best-known paintings.

Maine's Artists

One group of people who have never been in short supply in Maine is artists. Writers, painters, and many other kinds of artists have always been drawn to the spectacular landscapes and fascinating traditions of the Pine Tree State. Many came to Maine from elsewhere, but a large number were born in the state.

Henry Wadsworth Longfellow, of Portland, is a famous American poet. Other well-known Maine poets include Edna St. Vincent Millay of Rockland and Edward Arlington Robinson, who was born in Head Tide. E. B. White, author of *Charlotte's Web* and *Stuart Little*, left New York City to spend the last twenty-eight years of his life on a farm in North Brooklin. Maine's most popular living writer is Stephen King. He spends much of his year in Bangor. Maine also gave Hollywood one of its most respected directors—John Ford. Born in Cape Elizabeth, Ford won six Academy Awards in his lifetime. He is known for his classic Westerns, which often starred the legendary John Wayne.

Painters, too, have always been drawn to Maine, and especially to the breathtaking scenery of the seacoast. Winslow Homer, one of the most famous artists of nineteenth-century America, spent many years depicting the state's seascapes. In the mid-twentieth century, Rockwell Kent became famous for his paintings of Monhegan Island, where he lived for many years. Members of the Wyeth family, including N. C., Andrew, and Jamie, have been painting in Maine for almost a hundred years.

No matter where they are from or what they do, Mainers are proud to call the state their home. Its beautiful land, expanding cities, quality schools, charming towns, and good-hearted people all make the Pine Tree State a great place to live.

Maine painter N. C. Wyeth created illustrations for *Treasure Island,* by Robert Louis Stevenson. This 2011 exhibit featured all of Wyeth's paintings for the book.

Calendar of Events

★ National Toboggan Championships

During the first weekend in February, Camden plays host to hundreds of thrill-seeking tobogganers. The heart-stopping dash down the 400-foot (122-m) toboggan "chute" takes about 10 seconds and much courage.

★ Maine Maple Sunday

On the fourth Sunday in March, sugarhouses all over the state open their doors to visitors. Many houses offer demonstrations of making syrup from tree sap as well as free samples of the sweet treat.

★ Windjammer Days

For one weekend in June, Boothbay Harbor is crowded with windjammers and other "tall ships" for a celebration of the region's maritime history.

★ Acadian Festival

The largest cultural festival in Maine happens every summer, in Madawaska, near the Canadian border. Acadian art, music, and food is featured. Every year, the highlight of the festival is a huge reunion of one of Maine's pioneering Acadian families.

★ Maine Lobster Festival

Every August, some 100,000 lobster lovers descend on Rockland. They come to enjoy parades, music, and, of course, thousands of pounds of lobster.

★ Maine Wild Blueberry Festival

The sweetest place in all of Maine may just be the little town of Union. Union celebrates the August blueberry harvest with muffins, pastries, and a pie-eating contest.

★ Common Ground Country Fair

This "celebration of rural living" has been held in Unity every September since 1977. Hosted by the Maine Organic Farmers and Gardeners Association (MOFGA), the fair features food from local farms, animal exhibits, and crafts. Each year, MOFGA holds a poster design contest to choose the image that will represent the fair. The posters are a popular collector's item.

★ Harvestfest

Autumn is a wonderful time to visit the historic village of York, which celebrates the coming of autumn with traditional Maine crafts, wagon rides, and a corn-toss contest.

How the Government Works

The famous independent spirit of the Pine Tree State means the people of Maine make up their own minds. When they want something to happen, they often make it happen themselves.

Like all states, Maine is represented in the federal government by two U.S. senators, who serve six-year terms in Washington, D.C. The state is also represented by two members of the House of Representatives, according to the state's population as measured in the 2010 Census. The population of a state determines the number of people that it sends to the U.S. House of Representatives. Every state must have at least one member in the House. Members of the House of Representatives serve two-year terms.

The Maine constitution, which was adopted in 1820, divides the state government into three separate but equal branches: executive, legislative, and judicial. This arrangement creates a balance of powers, to prevent any one branch from becoming too powerful.

Quick Facts

AMERICAN INDIAN TOWNSHIPS

There are three American Indian townships in Maine. These townships have their own tribal governments. They are each led by a governor, lieutenant governor, and tribal council. An elected tribal representative from each township serves in Maine's state legislature.

The state capitol, in Augusta, was completed in 1832. Its dome is topped by a statue of Minerva, the Roman goddess of wisdom.

Residents of Rome sing the national anthem at the opening of their annual town meeting.

The people elected to represent Maine are often every bit as independent as the people who sent them there. But it is at the local level that Maine's unique brand of self-government shows most clearly. Maine has 16 counties, 22 cities, and 435 towns. Under a special form of government called home rule, each local area has the right to choose its own form of local government.

Some of Maine's cities and towns have an elected mayor and a city or town council. These officials make important decisions about the management of the area. But most of Maine's communities are run by representatives called selectmen (even though they can be either men or women). The selectmen handle the day-to-day running of the town. But the most important decisions are made at a town meeting.

The town meeting has been a New England tradition for hundreds of years. Once a year, all the residents of a town can come to the annual meeting, to

Branches of Government

EXECUTIVE ★ ★ ★ ★ ★ ★ ★ ★

The executive branch, headed by the governor, makes sure that the state's laws are carried out properly and handles the day-to-day running of the state government. The governor is elected by all the voters of the state, in elections held every four years, and can serve no more than two terms in a row. There is no limit on the total number of terms a governor can serve, however.

LEGISLATIVE ★ ★ ★ ★ ★ ★ ★ ★

The Maine legislature is divided into two houses, or chambers: the senate and the house of representatives, which meet at the State House in Augusta. The 35 members of the senate and the 151 members of the house of representatives create new laws and change existing ones. They are elected by their local districts and serve for two-year terms. They can serve no more than four terms in a row.

JUDICIAL ★ ★ ★ ★ ★ ★ ★ ★

The judicial branch is the court system. It settles legal disputes, punishes people who commit crimes, and decides whether Maine's laws violate the state constitution. The state's highest court, the Supreme Judicial Court, handles the most serious cases, constitutional issues, and appeals from lower courts. This court is made up of a chief justice and six associate judges. Maine's next highest court is the superior court, which handles all cases requiring a jury trial. The state also has district and probate courts. These courts handle trials without juries and civil trials involving relatively small amounts of money. All of Maine's judges are appointed by the state's governor, and serve terms of seven years. There is no limit on the number of terms they may serve.

discuss and vote on the most important local political issues. This is one of the oldest forms of "direct democracy" in the world. Direct democracy means that people have a chance to vote on important issues themselves. It gives everyone in the town a voice in their government. Between meetings, an elected board supervises town decisions.

In the past, just about everybody came to the town meeting, which is usually held in March. Attendance has dropped off in recent years, however, as most

The state capitol in Augusta is open to the public for tours.

town meetings are now televised live. Decisions about how to run the town and how to spend its money are made at town meetings, or voted on by secret ballot after the meeting is over. Common issues include dog leash laws, contracts for snow removal, and town budgets. The results of the meetings are often published in local newspapers.

How a Bill Becomes a Law

The process of creating a new state law is a slow, careful one. A new Maine law begins as an idea that is sponsored by a member of either house of the state legislature. The member proposes the creation of a new law, and lawyers, researchers, and other legislature staff help write a draft version. This draft is called a bill.

The legislator who sponsored the bill gives it to either the clerk of the house or the secretary of the senate, depending on his or her chamber. Each bill is referred to a joint standing committee. Each of these committees

A YOUNG AMBASSADOR FOR PEACE

The Cold War, which lasted for most of the second half of the twentieth century, was a time of competition between the United States and the Union of Soviet Socialist Republics (USSR) for power and influence in the world. At the height of the Cold War, in 1982, one young Mainer spoke up. Samantha Smith, a ten-year-old girl from Manchester, wrote a letter to Soviet leader Yuri Andropov about her fear of nuclear war. He responded personally and invited her to visit the USSR in 1983. Smith accepted his invitation and became known as one of her country's youngest ambassadors for peace. Tragically, Smith was killed in a plane crash in 1985, at the age of just thirteen, along with her father, Arthur Smith.

Samantha Smith, sitting between her parents, speaks with reporters in 1983.

considers bills on a certain topic. If the bill is related to schools, for example, it would be referred to the joint standing committee on education and cultural affairs. The committee holds a public hearing to hear supporting and opposing arguments from the public. Then, the committee decides whether to suggest passing the bill as is, passing with changes (or amendments), or not passing it at all.

If the majority of the committee members support the bill, it is opened for debate within the full house or senate, with two formal readings. If the first chamber approves the bill, it goes to the other body of the legislature to be considered. Both houses must agree on the exact same wording of the bill.

Sometimes the house and senate may have made different amendments to the bill. In those cases, it is sent to a conference committee. The committee will try to find a middle ground that both houses can agree on. Once a final bill is agreed upon by the house and senate, it goes to the governor.

If the governor signs the bill, it becomes law. However, the governor may refuse to sign it. This is called a veto, and it keeps the law from taking effect. The legislature can override this veto, with a two-thirds' majority vote in both houses. If it does, the bill becomes a law even though the governor disagrees with it.

Making a Difference

If there is a political issue that you care about, you can make a difference. Many of Maine's laws were created because ordinary Mainers wanted them.

The first step is to make sure you are well informed about all sides of the issues. You can do this by reading your local newspaper, in print or online, and following the local and national news. Your school and local libraries can help you stay informed, too, by recommending resources about topics that interest you.

The next thing to do is to find out how to contact your elected representatives. You can find the leaders of your local government—the mayor, the city council members, or the selectmen—online. Most state governments have websites that list names, addresses, telephone numbers, and e-mail addresses of their political leaders and, sometimes, how they voted on proposed bills. All you need to know to find your legislator is your city, town, or county.

Now that you know who your representatives are, it is time to make your voice heard. If you live in a town that holds an annual town meeting, you can attend it, even if you are not old enough to vote. It can be interesting to hear your neighbors talk about the issues that matter most to them—especially when those issues affect you, too.

Contacting Lawmakers

★ ★ ★ ★ ★ ★ ★ ★ ★ ★ ★ ★ ★

To find contact information for Maine's state legislators, go to

http://www.maine.gov/portal/ government/edemocracy/ lookup_voter_info

Choose your city or town, then type in your address to find your state senator and representative.

Quick Facts

A MAINE LEADER

One of Maine's best-known political figures is George Mitchell, born in Waterville in 1933. After attending Bowdoin College in Brunswick, he practiced law in Portland and later became a judge. Mitchell was appointed to the U.S. Senate in 1980 and was elected to the seat in 1982. From 1989 to 1995, he served as Senate majority leader. Senator Mitchell led a successful reauthorization of the Clean Air Act and helped pass the Americans with Disabilities Act. Later, Mitchell worked under President Bill Clinton as special adviser to the peace process in Northern Ireland and under President Barack Obama as a special envoy to the Middle East. Mitchell's contributions toward world peace have been recognized with several major awards, including the United Nations (UNESCO) Peace Prize.

Making a Living

Mainers have always been hardworking, because Maine can be a tough place to make a living. That has been especially true in the past few years as jobs in some parts of Maine have decreased. The northern parts of the state have been hit particularly hard. By the end of 2011, the unemployment rate for all of Maine was 7.3 percent. Although that number was more than a percentage point lower than the national average, in remote Washington County, in the northeastern corner of the state, the number was much higher.

Manufacturing

Manufacturing is an important segment of the Maine economy. But in the past few years, manufacturing industries have been badly hurt all across Maine. In the 1950s and 1960s, half of all Maine workers were employed in manufacturing, making such things as wood products, textiles, and shoes. Today, only about 9 percent of Mainers work in the manufacturing sector. That number will probably fall even lower in the years to come.

Wood products are the most important of Maine's manufactured goods. The state ships Christmas trees and wreaths, plywood, and shingles all over the world. Maine also produces more toothpicks than any other state. The most important of Maine's wood products is pulp and paper. This industry, too, is suffering, with some mills closing and workers losing their jobs.

Lobster fishing is still an important part of Maine's economy.

Workers & Industries

Industry	Number of People Working in That Industry	Percentage of All Workers Who Are Working in That Industry
Education and health care	180,987	28.2%
Wholesale and retail businesses	101,393	15.8%
Publishing, media, entertainment, hotels, and restaurants	65,421	10.2%
Manufacturing	59,100	9.2%
Professionals, scientists, and managers	56,888	8.9%
Construction	42,829	6.7%
Banking and finance, insurance, and real estate	39,599	6.2%
Government	28,280	4.4%
Other services	27,603	4.3%
Transportation and public utilities	24,250	3.8%
Farming, fishing, forestry, and mining	15,315	2.4%
Totals	641,665	100%

Notes: Figures above do not include people in the armed forces. "Professionals" includes people such as doctors and lawyers.

Source: U.S. Bureau of the Census, 2010 estimates

One of the main reasons for this decline is foreign competition. Maine's manufacturers must now compete with products from other countries where workers' wages are lower and goods are often much cheaper to make.

Beginning in the 1990s, the shipyards of Bath and Kittery laid off many employees. This decline in the shipbuilding industry did not happen because of competition from other countries. The problem was that, in a time of peace, the U.S. military was not ordering as many ships.

From the Land and Water

It might seem surprising that Maine, with its rocky soil and short growing season, has any agriculture at all. But farming is quite important in some areas of the state. Farms in different parts of the state produce oats, hay, and corn. Most of these crops are used to make food for livestock. Aroostook County produces potatoes and broccoli. The Augusta area is well known for its apple farms. Other parts of Maine produce blueberries and maple syrup. Maine produces more blueberries than any other state, and it is second in the nation for maple syrup production.

Maine does not have a very large mining industry, but there are some valuable mined products. The Pine Tree State has sand, gravel, and limestone, which are used in construction. Copper and zinc can be found in northern parts of Maine, but they are not usually mined in large quantities. The state mineral,

Though Maine's shipbuilding industry has declined in recent years, the Portsmouth Naval Shipyard continues to employ many residents.

RECIPE FOR MAINE BLUEBERRY PUDDING

This traditional Maine recipe is simple to make and delicious. You can use any kind of blueberries. If you can find lowbush blueberries from Maine—either fresh, frozen, or canned, give them a try.

WHAT YOU NEED

3 cups (450 grams) blueberries

1 teaspoon (5 g) cinnamon

$^3/_4$ cup (150 g) sugar

$^1/_2$ cup (120 ml) water

6 bread slices, with crusts removed

Whipped cream or ice cream

Mix together the blueberries, cinnamon, sugar, and water in a large saucepan. Have an adult help you cook the mixture on the stove. Bring the mixture to a boil over medium heat. Cook for about 10 minutes, stirring occasionally, until the berries have softened slightly.

While the blueberry mixture cools, line the bottom of a loaf pan with a layer of bread slices. If necessary, cut the slices to make a snug fit. Put about one-third of the blueberry mixture on top, and then add another layer of bread.

Continue until you have three layers of blueberry and bread. Chill the pan in the refrigerator overnight, or for 6 to 8 hours.

Cut into slices when the pudding is firm, top with whipped cream or ice cream, and enjoy!

tourmaline, is mined and made into jewelry that is sold all over the world. The mineral was first discovered at Mount Mica in 1820.

Maine's fishing industry is an important part of the economy. Since the first settlements, boats and ships have gone into Maine's inland and coastal waters to catch fish and crustaceans. The fishing industry also includes the people who clean, prepare, pack, and ship the fish and crustaceans throughout the country and around the world.

But lately, the stocks of ocean fish such as cod and haddock have decreased. Maine's fishing industry is regulated by a U.S. government agency called the National Marine Fisheries Service (NMFS). The agency has cut back on the numbers of fish that commercial fishers are allowed to catch. While this protects the fish populations, it has made it difficult for many of Maine's fishers to make a living.

The state's lobster population continues to flourish, however. In 2010, Maine's yearly lobster catch was about 93 million pounds (42 million kg). This catch, worth more than $308 million, was an increase from previous years. Other New England states have seen a decrease in the size of their lobster harvest due to rising water temperatures. So far, the coastal areas north of Cape Cod, Massachusetts, have been spared. "Lobstering's hard work," says a master boat and house builder in Spruce Head. "You'll head out at four o'clock in the morning, in all kinds of weather, and you might not [get] in till eight o'clock at night. But it's a good life, and you can make a good living."

A Maine fisher prepares his lobster traps, or pots, for another day on the water.

Products & Resources

Tourism

Tourism is big business in Maine. In the summer of 2010, more than 23 million people visited the state. People from all over the world come to experience the state's cities, museums, historical sites, restaurants, coastal resorts, and parks.

Potatoes

Maine is the eighth-largest potato-growing state in the country. Almost 55,000 acres (22,260 ha) of Maine farmland—mostly in Aroostook County—produced more than $159 million of potatoes in 2010.

Lobster

Lobster was so plentiful in Maine's early days that it was called "poverty food"—something even the poorest people could afford to eat. Today, it is one of the world's most expensive foods. More than 80 percent of the lobsters served in the entire country come from the cold, clear waters off the Maine coast.

Blueberries

Wild lowbush blueberries—smaller and more flavorful than farm-produced highbush blueberries—grow beautifully in Maine's thin, rocky soil. In 2010, the state produced 83 million pounds (38 million kg) of blueberries.

Pulp and Paper

Wood products—from sailboats to toothpicks and everything in between—are an important part of the manufacturing industry. The state's mills produce approximately 4 million tons (3.6 million metric tons) of paper every year.

Dairy Farms

At one time, Maine had more than five thousand dairy farms throughout the state. Today, however, there are only about three hundred. But the products from these farms are still important to Maine. The milk from Maine's dairy cows is made into cream, butter, ice cream, and cheese. Dairy farmers also sell their cow manure to become part of rich fertilizers for sale throughout the state and around the country.

ANDRE THE SEAL

In 1961, a tree surgeon named Harry Goodridge found an abandoned harbor seal pup off the coast of Rockport. He kept the seal, named Andre, in a floating pen, where he would perform tricks for visitors, in the summer and let the seal swim free in the winter. Unfortunately, Andre became so comfortable with people that he approached them for food and climbed on to boats. For Andre's safety, Goodridge began shipping him to aquariums in Connecticut or Boston, Massachusetts. When he was released every summer, Andre would swim back to Rockport. This ritual continued until Andre's death in 1986. His story was told in several children's books and a 1994 movie, *Andre*. Today, a statue of Andre is one of Rockport's most popular tourist attractions.

Services and Tourism

The service industry includes any jobs that provide a service to others. Teachers, doctors, tour guides, waiters, and hotel clerks are all part of the service industry. The service industry employs a large number of Mainers.

Tourism is one of the most profitable parts of Maine's service industry. The Pine Tree State has something for just about every visitor. This includes the spectacular beauty of the seacoast, the unspoiled wilderness in the interior—including 436,064 square miles (1,129,401 sq km) of national and state parks—and the peaceful, easygoing Maine way of life.

But part of what brings tourists to Maine is the people. Mainers offer visitors a friendly "down east" welcome that keeps them coming back, year after year. And that makes tourism one Maine industry that keeps growing, no matter how troubled the economy might be.

New Ways

Maine still relies heavily on its traditional industries and natural resources, such as wood and fish. It is working hard to develop modern, advanced industries, however. Financial services have become an important part of the Maine economy, as banks and insurance companies have moved their headquarters into the state. More and more technology industries, such as software companies, are moving into Maine, especially around Portland.

Businesses are choosing to come to Maine for many reasons. The state has a fairly low cost of living, with inexpensive places to live. Traveling to and from Maine is easy, thanks to its two international airports and frequent trains and buses to Boston and New York City. Another bonus for industries and employers is the well-educated, highly skilled workforce.

The University of Southern Maine, which has its main campus in Gorham, is part of the University of Maine System.

Maine's workforce is often educated at the state's excellent colleges and universities. The University of Maine System (UMS) is made up of seven universities, including its flagship school, the University of Maine in Orono. More than 11,000 students attend UMaine Orono, which was founded in 1862. Maine is also known for such prestigious private colleges as Bates, Bowdoin, and Colby.

People have always had to work hard to get by in Maine, often taking on more than one job. A fisher would work as a carpenter in the winter, when it was too cold to go out on the water. A farmer might have a job in town to help make ends meet. It is this spirit—hardworking, independent, and resourceful—that has always carried Mainers through good times and bad. And it is this spirit that makes the people of Maine by far the state's most important natural resource.

State Flag & Seal

The Maine state flag, chosen in 1909, shows the state seal, against a blue background. The background is the same shade of blue as in the flag of the United States.

The state seal shows some of the people and resources that have been important throughout Maine's history. A farmer and a sailor stand on either side of a shield showing a pine tree and a moose. Above the shield is the state's motto, Dirigo, which means "I lead." Below is the word Maine.

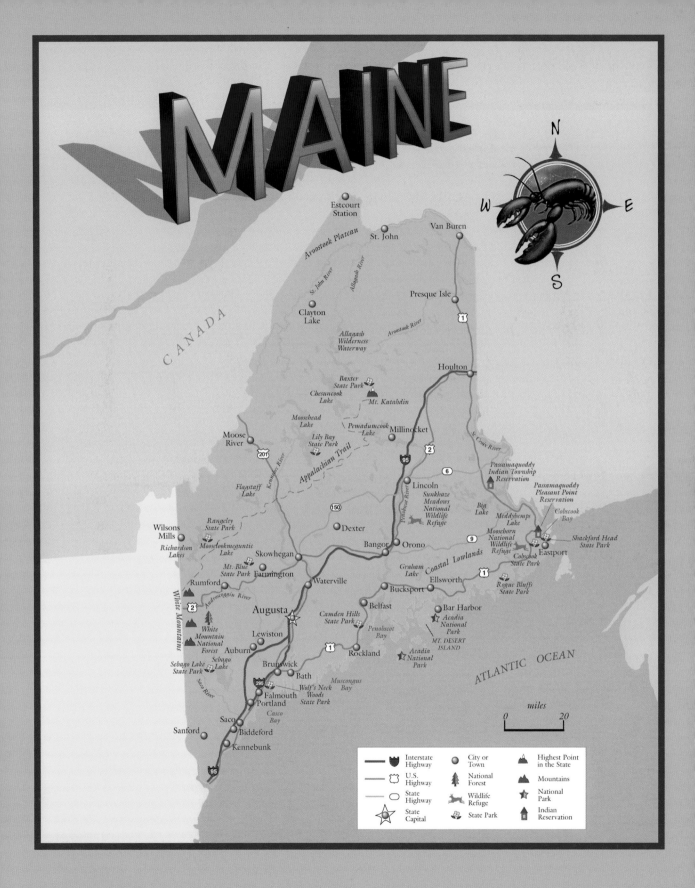

MAINE

N
W · E
S

Estcourt
Station

St. John

Van Buren

Aroostook Plateau

St. John River

Allagash River

Presque Isle

1

Clayton
Lake

*Allagash
Wilderness
Waterway*

Aroostook River

Houlton

*Baxter
State Park*

*Chesuncook
Lake*

Mt. Katahdin

*Moosehead
Lake*

*Pemadumcook
Lake*

Millinocket

*Lily Bay
State Park*

95

Moose
River

201

Kennebec River

Appalachian Trail

St. Croix River

Passamaquoddy
Indian Township
Reservation

Lincoln

2

6

*Flagstaff
Lake*

150

*Sunkhaze
Meadows
National
Wildlife
Refuge*

Big
Lake

*Meddybemps
Lake*

Passamaquoddy
Pleasant Point
Reservation

Cobscook
Bay

Wilsons
Mills

*Rangeley
State Park*

Dexter

Bangor

Orono

9

*Moosehorn
National
Wildlife
Refuge*

Eastport

Shackford Head
State Park

*Richardson
Lakes*

*Mooselookmeguntic
Lake*

Skowhegan

*Graham
Lake*

Coastal Lowlands

*Cobscook
State Park*

*Mt. Blue
State Park*

Farmington

Waterville

Ellsworth

1

*Roque Bluffs
State Park*

Rumford

Androscoggin River

Bucksport

Bar Harbor

2

Augusta

*Camden Hills
State Park*

Belfast

*Acadia
National
Park*

*White
Mountains*

*White
Mountain
National
Forest*

Lewiston

Auburn

*Penobscot
Bay*

*MT. DESERT
ISLAND*

*Sebago Lake
State Park*

*Sebago
Lake*

Brunswick

1

Rockland

*Acadia
National
Park*

Saco River

Bath

*Muscongus
Bay*

ATLANTIC OCEAN

295

*Wolf's Neck
Woods
State Park*

Falmouth
Portland

*Casco
Bay*

miles
0   20

Saco

Sanford

Biddeford

Kennebunk

95

CANADA

	Interstate Highway		City or Town		Highest Point in the State
	U.S. Highway		National Forest		Mountains
	State Highway		Wildlife Refuge		National Park
	State Capital		State Park		Indian Reservation

State Song

State of Maine Song

words and music by Roger Vinton Snow

BOOKS

Baughan, Michael Gray. *Stephen King*. New York: Chelsea House, 2009.

Elliot, Henry. *Harriet Beecher Stowe: The Voice of Humanity in White America*. New York: Crabtree, 2010.

Graham, Amy. *Acadia National Park: Adventure, Explore, Discover*. Berkeley Heights, NJ: MyReportLinks.com Books, 2009.

House, Katherine L. *Lighthouses for Kids: History, Science, and Lore with 21 Activities*. Chicago: Chicago Review Press, 2008.

Perkins, Wendy. *Maine Coon Cats*. Mankato, MN: Capstone Press, 2008.

WEBSITES

Maine Historical Society:
http://www.mainehistory.org

Maine Office of Tourism:
http://www.visitmaine.com

Maine Official State Website:
http://www.maine.gov

Secretary of State's Kids' Page:
http://www.state.me.us/sos/kids

Terry Allan Hicks has written books about the states of New Hampshire and Nevada. He lives in Connecticut with his wife, Nancy, and their children, Jamie, Jack, and Andrew.

Amanda Hudson is a writer and editor who grew up in the small town of Readfield, Maine. She now lives with her husband outside of New York City but travels back to Maine whenever possible for lobster rolls, mosquito bites, and white Christmases with her family.

★ INDEX ★

Page numbers in **boldface** are illustrations.